THE LIFE AND WISDOM OF

AUGUSTINE
OF HIPPO

THE 'SAINTS ALIVE' SERIES

THE LIFE AND WISDOM OF

AUGUSTINE

OF HIPPO

———— ◆ ————

Written and Compiled by
LAVINIA BYRNE

Hodder & Stoughton
LONDON   SYDNEY   AUCKLAND

British Library Cataloguing in Publication Data:
A record for this book is available from the British Library.

ISBN 0 340 70971 5

Typeset in Monotype Columbus by
Strathmore Publishing Services, London N7.

Printed and bound in Great Britain by
Mackays of Chatham PLC, Chatham, Kent.

Hodder and Stoughton Ltd,
A division of Hodder Headline PLC,
338 Euston Road, London NW1 3BH

CONTENTS

INTRODUCTION

Who are the saints and why should we bother to
know about their lives? We are inclined to think
of them as heroic people who did extraordinary
things, or as people who suffered a great deal
and were somehow specially gifted or good.
What we then forget is that, in general, saints are
people like us. They struggled to know themselves better, to be more kind and loving, more
self-accepting, less neurotic. They did not always
succeed. They thought their attempts to live with
integrity would make them closer to other people and to God. Often what they then discovered
was that other people became harder to love and
that God simply disappeared.

Yet they kept up the struggle. They believed
that they were given one chance, that they had to
live with a certain generosity, because this life is
a preparation for the full glory of the next life.
They then learnt that we are given many chances

because all is grace, and the Christian life is a life of grace. So their schemes and plans for being holy were dismantled. All that was asked of them was a readiness to accept the gifts of God, including the final gift of heaven.

Saints come from every walk of life. They are men and women who share our concerns about money, power, politics, peace, energy, food, war, death, sex, love, privacy, the inner life, the outer life, harmony, balance. What makes them distinctive is that they looked beyond themselves to know how best to live and they discovered that God shared their concerns. If we read about them nowadays, we do so out of more than simple curiosity. Their lives are worth reading because we can learn from them. We look for more than a good example, though. The saints seem to know more than we do; they have access to a deeper level of wisdom than our own. They are gurus for our times. So when we read about them, we are quite right to seek an insight into the mind of God, who calls and inspires us all to the heroism of holiness, however we ourselves happen to live. Holiness is for all, not just the few; for a holy life is no more than a life lived in the presence of God.

In our materialistic and agnostic age, do the saints still matter? Have they any wisdom for us, or are they simply a pious irrelevance? Are their lives mere legends or do they have some significance beyond the bare bones of what history tells us about them? Augustine is one of the most attractive and elusive of the saints, for he is a man who went on a journey, and his journey brought him inexorably into the presence of God. The route meanwhile was baffling, complex. It led him to experience his own capacity for error and for sin. It led him to clamour for forgiveness and to find true rest only in the knowledge and love of God. He fathered an illegitimate son and then, on his conversion, abandoned the child's mother. He took risks, trying out different lifestyles until he found the one that worked for him.

Augustine dared to ask questions of God and of his own experience, grappling to know the truth. His struggles were ferocious, as he fought with other people and within himself. He was the first modern man, someone who wrote out his own story in his *Confessions*, someone who wrestled to understand his motivation, dreams and the life of his unconscious. The life of Augustine was a fascinating and a troubled one. It forces us to ask ourselves where our own true rest lies; it supplies us with a compelling set of answers.

PART ONE

The Story of His Early Years

'Take and read; take and read'

PART ONE

'Take and read; take and read'

A voice in the garden
'*Tolle, lege; tolle, lege.*' Augustine was in a garden
in Milan when he heard these words. A child
was singing beyond the neighbouring wall.
'Take and read', the nursery rhyme rang out like
a challenge. A man of thirty-two, Augustine had
been agonising over the direction his life should
take. He was drawn to change his ways, which
had been dissolute, but was also repelled by the
demands such a change might ask of him. He
had been promiscuous in his youth, selfish and
wayward, intellectually questioning and arro-
gant by turns. He had ignored the feelings of
the people closest to him – his mother and his
mistress. Had he cheated and lied and grabbed
his way to fame and glory as a teacher and
rhetorician?

Then, on an August afternoon in AD 386 in

1

Milan, a child's voice floated over from the next-door garden: 'Take and read; take and read.' This refrain from a nursery song called out to Augustine. He turned to the scriptures, opened the book which he had just been looking at, a collection of Paul's epistles, and lit on the words, 'Let us live honourably as in the day, not in revelling and drunkenness, not in debauchery and licentiousness, not in quarrelling and jealousy. Instead, put on the Lord Jesus Christ, and make no provision for the flesh, to gratify its desire' (Romans 13.13–14). With this message, his eyes were opened and he experienced the grace of forgiveness. God spoke to him in a sudden and unexpected way. The teacher was unmanned as he learnt from the voice of a child.

Augustine takes up the story in his *Confessions*, telling God what happened:

We went inside and told my mother, who was overjoyed. When we related to her how it had happened she was filled with triumphant delight and blessed you, who have power to do more than we ask or understand for she saw that you had granted her much more in my regard than she had been wont to beg of you in her wretched, tearful groaning. Many years earlier you had shown her a vision of me standing on the rule of faith; and now indeed I stood there, no longer seeking a wife or entertaining any worldly hope, for you have converted me to yourself. In so doing you had also converted her grief into joy far more abundant than she had desired, and much more tender and chaste than she could ever have looked to find in grandchildren from my flesh.

The context

Who are the characters in this drama? Why is Augustine so ridden with grief and guilt? What are the issues? Augustine was thirty-two when he was converted to Christianity. He had been born in Thagaste in Numidia on 13 November 354. The town is now called Souk-Arras, in modern Algeria. When Augustine was born, it was part of the Roman Empire. Everywhere he would have seen signs of Roman influence: roads, baths, aqueducts, columns, hippodromes, a forum and a theatre. Each of these was a monument set in stone of the prevailing images, ideas and metaphors which would govern his life. He thought he would live on a stage like a rhetorician. He journeyed mentally and emotionally, as well as on the roads of the Roman Empire. He was eventually bathed in a baptismal font which brought him the waters of life, as he saw it, rather than those delivered to the baths of Thagaste by the aqueduct. The city faced south and was built on a promontory two thousand feet above sea level. The view presented signs of stability and prosperity: olive groves, corn fields and farm animals, for the province exported oil, corn and hides to Rome. The Punic Wars between Rome and Africa had ended in 146 with the destruction of Carthage. A new westernised Africa emerged, divided into three regions and, with intermarriage, the Berbers or native people became amalgamated with their Roman colonisers. The Empire's days were numbered, but here in North Africa, it still presented itself in its full splendour, with a stable and relatively prosperous community enjoying the benefits of belonging to a wider world with open trade routes and a secure currency.

Augustine's parents were poor but free, not slaves. Patricius, his father, had married Monica, his mother, some ten years before Augustine's birth. She was a devout Christian, while her husband, as was commonly the case at the time, converted only in the year of his death, 370. When he was born Augustine was blessed with the sign of the cross, but not baptised. As a child he enjoyed playing, but he was bright and his parents decided to make the kind of sacrifices which would enable him to receive a good education. Such an education would guarantee his escape from the little world of Thagaste. He engaged in all the scrapes of childhood and adolescence. He spoke Latin, loved Virgil and hated Homer. We know these details because of the book he wrote, his *Confessions*. His book is addressed to God, whom he calls 'you' and to whom he writes the story of his life. His *Confessions* are the world's first autobiography. To write your own story is an extraordinarily modern concept, but then Augustine was an extraordinarily modern man.

His concerns are our concerns; his interests our own. He worried about the things which still worry us: his desires, his dreams, his lack of will power, his inability to take control. He does not simply tell his own story, he explores his own psycho-drama. Few people have written their story with this degree of honesty, setting the record straight with God and other people.

The book's title is significant. For Augustine writes his autobiography as an act of self-revelation. He wants to tell his story, to confess what he did with his life, to tell us about the shame and the glory of it all. But equally he wants to tell us about God, to confess or profess his belief in the absoluteness of God and the experience he had of forgiveness from God. So the book becomes a kind of prayer, an extended conversation with God, a lyrical assertion of the right of God to be known and heard and believed in. He uses the language of the Psalms to pour out his soul but also, as a philosopher, he includes a great deal of original speculation about creation and time and chance. His life was turned around by the force and power of divine love and so he writes directly to us and for us as he tells the story of the workings of grace in his life.

The story

The story is a simple one, as simple and as shaming as any of our stories when they are exposed to the gaze of forgiveness and love. Once his primary education was completed, his parents sent the boy to Madaura, some twenty-five miles south of Thagaste. There he studied until he was sixteen. Then he came home for a year, before going off to Carthage for further studies. This idle year did him no good at all. 'Love and lust boiled within me,' he would later write. He implies that he tried everything, because he was a total prey to his feelings. The only fact which he gives, however, sounds relatively harmless. With friends, he stripped a neighbour's pear tree of all its fruit. Perhaps this incident encapsulated all the wildness and wantonness that he experienced at this time.

The following year, his parents had raised enough money to send him off to study in

Carthage. His father converted and died, while Monica continued to pray for her wayward son. He, meanwhile, had taken up with an unnamed concubine, one of history's more invisible women, for we know nothing about her. The following year, his son, Adeodatus, was born. The boy's name means 'Given to God'. Augustine lived with the boy's mother for the next fifteen years, teaching first in Carthage, then in Rome in 383 and finally in Milan in 384.

These bald facts mask a turbulent reality, for Augustine was also exploring ideas as well as feelings during this period. The feelings are understandable. Here was a turbulent young man, bright and bent on self-discovery. Here was a boy who was deeply normal, but equally who was deeply sensitive to the meaning of his own experience. He could not let it go. He repeatedly revisited it to try to pull out the deeper meaning of what he was doing. Here was a man who was being prepared for a deeper destiny.

We do not know the name of his mistress but we may assume that she brought stability into his life because theirs became a stable relationship.

The birth of their son was not seen as a tragedy or an embarrassment but rather as an indication of this security. Augustine loved Adeodatus and kept the boy with him wherever he travelled. For now the travelling began in earnest.

Carthage, Rome, Milan

When he set off to study at Carthage on the north coast of Africa, Augustine was moving up in the world. He was planning to be a lawyer and only changed his studies to philosophy when he got there. Carthage was larger and more sophisticated than Thagaste. It boasted an amphitheatre for twenty thousand people and huge public baths. At the university Augustine began to read Cicero's *Hortensius*. This book made him aspire to think about wisdom in a new way and to centre his life on a search for truth and other absolutes. He tried reading the Bible at about this time, but found its stories too simple and uninteresting to hold his attention. The pursuit of a higher ideal seemed more important to him. In fairness, it should be added that the version of the Bible which was available to him in North Africa was neither an accurate translation nor in good Latin; it gave him the impression that Christianity was an incoherent collection of fables which had neither moral spine nor intellectual rigour. These qualities were becoming increasingly important to him. He was actively in search of a belief system and of meaning.

In Carthage, Augustine was first exposed to the thinking of the Manichaeans. He embarked on one of the three journeys into self-discovery of his life. For by grappling with the thinking of this sect, he began to ask serious questions about reality. The Manichaeans were members of a religious group which had begun its life a century earlier, in Iran. They combined learning from a variety of different sources, choosing ideas from philosophy, from more primitive and superstitious sources with ones from Judaism and Christianity. They wanted to explain creation, the existence of good and evil, the meaning of life. What they offered Augustine was a philosophical framework. Mani the Persian, who originated the system, was highly successful in spreading a kind of universalised

Gnosticism, a 'pick 'n mix' religion, honouring Jesus and the Buddha, Zoroaster and other spiritual teachers, but rejecting the Old Testament. Mani thought he was a Christian, and Augustine probably believed, when he joined the cult, that it was true Christianity, only more sophisticated, more interesting than straight orthodoxy.

From the Manichaeans, Augustine got the idea that there was a fundamental battle between good and evil, and that God, though good, was not omnipotent. He was not responsible for evil, but neither could he overcome it. For Mani divided the universe into two kingdoms: one a kingdom of light, one a kingdom of matter or of darkness. This same system was replicated within every human being, with light represented by the spiritual side of people and darkness by their bodily reality. In common with many present-day sects, it was curiously hostile to the human spirit and deeply anti-materialistic.

The most perfect Manichaeans were the 'pure' or the 'elect', those who lived on a higher plane by the perfection of their lives. They abstained from meat and from evil words by having a 'seal' on their lips; from sex by having a 'seal' on their heart; and from unrighteous deeds by a 'seal' on their hands. Belief in reincarnation was fundamental to their understanding, as people clearly needed more than one life to become sufficiently pure to aspire to move to a higher, more celestial plane. Apart from the elect, there were also other adherents, known as 'hearers', who were not under such strict obligations. This is what Augustine became. The system offered security; hence its attraction to a clever mind, like that of the nineteen-year-old Augustine. He was to remain a Manichaean for the next nine years, only breaking free from its teachings as his mind began to be challenged by intellectual doubts. If human matter was so evil, he would come to ask, how could it carry the divine spark of the life of the spirit?

In 383 Augustine moved to the capital. Rome lured him with the promise of fame and glory. Here he hoped to make a reputation for himself as a teacher of philosophy and rhetoric. What he had not realised is that teachers in Rome were cheated by their students, who would leave lectures without paying. When the chance of a professorship in Milan came up the following year, he jumped at it.

Milan was a rich and bustling city. To get a decent job there and to advance his career, Augustine now needed money. For jobs were up for sale to the highest bidder. The best way to acquire money was to marry a rich wife. Now Augustine still had his mistress and Adeodatus, his son. But his mother Monica was working away in the background and had already found a suitable ten-year-old girl for him to marry in a few years' time. His mistress was despatched back to Carthage.

Augustine himself was always haunted by the loss of his first love, though in the *Confessions,* he speaks of her as his sin. She became associated in his mind with his youthful debauchery and loose living. In fact he was faithful to her for fifteen years and one wonders whether the language of guilt is not a disguise for the feelings of heart-break and grief which he was really experiencing. Augustine has had a bad press for his repressive attitude to sex and for never getting over his Manichaean past with its rigid divisions and codes of purity. In a later controversy, he would assert that sexual intercourse was the means by which original sin gets transmitted from one generation to the next. But he was a man of his time, and to disallow that is to do him no favours.

Nearly all the philosophers of the classical age were troubled by the irrationality and loss of control which they associated with the sexual act. For them it was not a source of liberation, but rather a sign of the disorderly aspects of human nature, to be handled with the greatest of care, and given up or renounced with a certain degree of relief. Perhaps this explains something about Augustine's attitude to women. In later life he did come to appreciate the wisdom and balance of his mother, Monica. But at no time could she be his intellectual friend and – as we shall see – friendship mattered greatly to him. She had not read the classics for she was not educated. Nor, of course, was his mistress. Yet one feels that he was constantly looking for a companion who would be his intellectual equal. He even went so far as to write, 'If God had wanted Adam to have a partner in conversation, he would have created another man.' The existence of women, in his mind, is totally tied up in the furtherance of the human race even though, in his writings on marriage, he insists that men and women are equal in body and spirit.

Augustine's mother Monica had been dismayed by his move to Rome, but now she followed him to Milan. Throughout the long years during which she had prayed for him to come to the true light of the gospel, she had not flagged. And her dream was to come true.

The conversion

For in Milan, Augustine found a man whose word and intelligence he respected. Ambrose, the Bishop of Milan, proved to be an important trigger to Augustine. He was a man who worked hard and Milan was the administrative centre of the Western Empire so he was influential. His own background was in administration. Indeed he was elected Bishop by popular demand, whilst still a civil servant. As Governor of Aemilia and Liguri, he had officiated at the congress called to elect a new bishop on the death of the previous one. A child's voice shouted out the words, 'Ambrose for Bishop', and within a week he had been baptised and consecrated. Children's voices were surprisingly influential in Milan.

Augustine came to hear him preach and was impressed. The Christian gospel began to exercise attraction for him. Unlike the teaching of the Manichaeans, it did not divide human experience into darkness and light. It reconciled the two. Unlike the teaching of the Manichaeans, it took sin seriously. Gradually Augustine was coming to see that sin is a consequence of the weakness of the human will. This required him to think more seriously about his own life and to take some responsibility for it. He was about to embark on the second journey of exploration in his life. Yet he did not move directly to Christianity, but came to it obliquely through the second step of his journey of conversion. For now he began to find comfort in the orderly ideas of Neoplatonism, as it too seemed to offer clarity and so enabled him to discover the deepest desires of his heart and will.

He may have joined a Neoplatonic reading group in Milan, men who met together to study the works of Plotinus. Plotinus had taught in Rome one hundred years previously. He was a great synthesiser of the different strands of Plato's thought which still circulated in the classical world, but he also added something of his own: a profound psychological insight into the place of the world in the Platonic vision. For Plotinus, at the heart of reality was The One, utterly simple, utterly good, the source of all that is, but beyond all categories, even being itself. This is a mystical vision of extraordinary simplicity. For everything comes from The One, as The One unfolds first into Intelligence, then into Soul, then into the multiplicity of being to which we, as human beings, belong. This outward flow from a still centre is balanced by a return as The One gathers or draws everything back to itself. Everything that is, even matter itself which is the weakest expression of the emanations from The

One, longs to return, to ascend or fold itself back to The One.

There is an inbuilt desire for a homecoming as we begin to journey back to The One. We begin this journey by turning inwards, by contemplation and self-knowledge, for as Augustine was about to discover, the ladder which leads to home is located in the self, not in some external place. The deepest and hardest journey is the journey within. Yet it alone can bring us to true clarity. So later, when Augustine writes to God in his *Confessions*, 'You were more inward than the inward place of my heart and loftier than the highest', he is echoing Plotinus.

There are other echoes, too, for Augustine risked humanising what he learnt. By translating these apparently cool and transcendental ideas into his own lived experience, he brought a depth of longing and keenly-felt emotions to theological reflection. For he understood homesickness and the power of an enfolding return to God. His was a questing, searching and ultimately a Christian heart.

So, inexorably, the stage was being set for the

fateful moment in the garden when the child's voice came sailing over the wall: 'Take and read; take and read', '*Tolle, lege; tolle, lege*'. Augustine's life would never be the same again. The restless journey of his quest for an absolute to live by was coming to an end. Later he would write, 'Thou hast made us for Thyself, O Lord, and our hearts are without rest until they learn to rest in Thee.'

The Christian heart

Where the Manichaeans had given him one frame of reference and Plotinus another, Augustine at the age of thirty-two began the third great spiritual journey of his life. He converted to Christianity. His first action was to go off to the country with his mother, his brother Navigius, two of his pupils – Trygetius and Licentius – his cousins Lastidianus and Rusticus, his friend Alypius and young Adeodatus, now aged fifteen. They were lent a house called Cassiciacum, near Lake Maggiore, a villa in the hills surrounded by chestnut and olive trees, with vineyards and fields a short walk away. For seven months he prepared for baptism, praying, reading the psalms, teaching and writing.

Augustine had been ill before this idyllic retreat to the country. His spirit was broken by the effort he had put into resisting conversion, but now he could flourish in the company of his family and friends, though he still had chest pains and difficulty in breathing. He began to realise that he wanted to devote himself to the service of God and that the life of seclusion had much to recommend itself to him. Here was peace; here was the possibility to grow in the knowledge and love of God; here was a perfect community. Of his mother at this time, Augustine wrote that she sat with them 'in the dress indeed of a woman, but with the faith of a man, the calmness of old age, the love of a mother, and the holiness of a Christian'. A rural idyll offered healing to Augustine's spirit.

At the beginning of Lent in 387, Augustine, Adeodatus and Alypius returned to Milan to prepare for baptism. They were duly baptised on Easter Eve by triple immersion in the name of the Father, Son and Holy Spirit. Ambrose himself

officiated at the ceremony and had shown a keen
interest in Augustine's acceptance of the gospel.
He wrote to him recommending that he read the
prophet Isaiah as part of his preparation.

Augustine's new life was now well and truly
launched. He planned to return home to Africa,
to abandon his career as a philosopher and to set
up a small community where he and his friends
and son could live the Christian life together. All
thoughts of marriage were abandoned. His life
would be dedicated to God. They set off to the
sea port of Ostia, planning their journey. At
Ostia, Monica and her son shared a particularly
close time together. One night, as they talked by
a window overlooking a small garden, Monica
spoke from the heart: 'My son, as far as I am concerned, nothing in this life delights me any
longer. What I am to do here, or why I am here,
I do not know, since for me the hope of this
world is spent. There was but one reason why I
desired to linger in this life a little longer. It was
that I might see you a Catholic Christian before
I died. My God has granted this to me in more
abundant measure, so that I even see you his

servant, despising all earthly happiness. What am I doing here?'

God must have heard this as a prayer for release for, five days later, Monica fell ill with a fever. She died on the ninth day of her illness, aged fifty-six. Her sons buried her in Ostia and returned to Rome to take stock. They were to live there for a year, while Augustine wrote, and then set off to return to Africa.

Faithful God,
who strengthened Monica, the mother of
    Augustine, with wisdom,
and through her patient endurance encouraged
    him to seek after you:
give us the will to persist in prayer
that those who stray from you may be brought
    to faith
in your Son Jesus Christ our Lord,
who is alive and reigns with you,
in the unity of the Holy Spirit,
one God, now and for ever.

– *Collect for the Feast of St Monica,*
The Christian Year

PART TWO

The Wisdom of Augustine

PART TWO

Religious life in Thagaste
The community at Cassiciacum had been a
community of scholars; in Thagaste, on his
return to his home town, Augustine set up a
community of holy men. Some of them were the
same friends who had been with him in Italy, like
his best friend Alypius; one was his son,
Adeodatus. A young man called Possidius joined
them, and observed that Augustine 'persevered
there for nearly three years, living for God in
fasting, prayer and good works, meditating day
and night on the laws of the Lord, and impart-
ing to others what God revealed to him during
contemplation and prayer'.

He wrote a book called *The Teacher*, a dia-
logue with Adeodatus. 'All the ideas which are
put in the mouth of the other party to the dia-
logue were truly his, though he was but sixteen,'

Augustine later wrote, and then he added, 'I had experience of many other remarkable qualities in him. His great intelligence filled me with a kind of awe, and who but God could have been the maker of things so wonderful? But you took him early from this earth and I think of him utterly without anxiety, for there is nothing in his boyhood or youth, or anywhere in him, to cause me to fear.' The date was probably 390, the cause of Adeodatus' death unknown. All the tenderness with which Monica loved her son is recognisable in the love and care which his father showed to Adeodatus, and privately mourned his loss.

This love was forged in a way of life which was both a religious and a theological preparation for the next stage in Augustine's journey, serving as a kind of combined noviciate and university. In the quiet of prayer and study, he was being trained for active service of the Church. Everything in his experience to date led him to believe that he would be a scholar and a writer. That would be the direction in which he should move. Yet the Church in Numidia had other and more complicated needs and these meshed even more closely with his gifts. Of course Augustine the theologian was critically significant to them, especially as he had been a Manichaean and so could deal directly with the threat such heretics posed to the orthodox Christian community, knowing the system, as he did, from the inside. But there was also Augustine the leader of men to think about, Augustine the loving father, the man of God and man of prayer. How could such a man best serve the Church?

The answer, to us, is blindingly obvious, but we are wise after the event. The words Augustine and Hippo are linked in our memories, however little we know of how he got to be bishop there. His own account is all the more telling for that very reason, for he was a reluctant bishop, not one who craved such a distinction.

The reputation of the community at Thagaste spread around Numidia. It was seen as a likely recruiting ground for bishops. Augustine dealt with this by a neat piece of strategy: he did not want to be a bishop, so he never went anywhere where there was an empty see. Instead he positively avoided such places. He later told his

congregation about his experience of coming to
Hippo one Sunday in 391. This account was
given thirty-four years later but his sense of
amazement sounds as fresh as it must have been
at the time:

I, whom you see, with God's grace, as your
bishop – I came as a young man to this city, as
many of you know. I was looking for a place to
set up a monastery, to live with my 'brethren'. I
had given up all hope in this world. What I
could have been, I wished not to be: nor did I
seek to be what I am now. For I chose to be
humble in the house of my God rather than to *live in
the tents of sinners.* I kept apart from those who
loved the world: but I did not think myself the
equal of those who ruled over congregations. At
the Lord's feast, I did not take up a higher
position, but chose a lower and more retiring
place: and it pleased the Lord to say, 'Rise up.'

I feared the office of a bishop to such an
extent that, as soon as my reputation came to
matter among 'servants of God', I would not go
to any place where I knew there was no bishop.

I was on my guard against this: I did what I could to seek salvation in a humble position rather than be in danger in high office. But, as I said, a slave cannot contradict his Lord. I came to this city to see a friend, whom I thought I might gain for God, that he might live with us in the monastery. I felt secure, for the place already had a bishop. I was grabbed. I was made a priest … and from there, I became your bishop.

So who was it who duped him on this memorable occasion? Valerius, the incumbent bishop, was an elderly man with a problem. As a Greek-speaker, he had little Latin, no Punic and no great gift for learning languages. Yet his church needed an articulate and authoritative teacher. No wonder he leapt upon Augustine as soon as he arrived in Hippo; no wonder Augustine was hurriedly ordained and promoted to high office by popular demand from the crowd. The episode is reminiscent of Ambrose's appointment in Milan, and Augustine's route to the episcopacy is at least as unorthodox. Valerius made him his co-adjutor bishop, a controversial move since the canons of the Council of Nicaea forbade more than one bishop in a diocese. Yet his strategy succeeded: Augustine followed Valerius as Bishop of Hippo in 396 and remained in North Africa until his death in 430.

The Hippo years

What was Hippo like when its new co-adjutor bishop arrived there? It was built on an inhospitable spot on the Mediterranean coast, facing north, with natural protection from mountains on the one hand and marshes on the other. Whatever remains of it nowadays is buried deep beneath a run-down Algerian city called Annaba. Yet here Augustine preached and prayed and taught his people for thirty-four years. Here he struggled with endless heretics and heresies on their behalf; here he fought their fights and arbitrated in their disputes, serving the church with all the generosity he could muster; here he acquired a range of experiences from which his Manichaean past would once upon a time have protected him. For in

Hippo Augustine became a man of the people
and a man of God.

A series of snapshots into his world is more
easily given by searching his sermons for evidence of what interested him than by searching
for archaeological remains, for he turned every-
day events into colourful anecdotes. He provides
his own archaeological sub-strata by talking
about oarsmen singing boat songs in unison on
the river, or birdcatchers imitating the call of
their quarry; jugglers dancing on a tightrope and
gamblers who get furious with their dice;
wealthy landowners who cannot sleep at night
for anxiety about their crops and hired hands
who are brought in to act as night-watchmen for
them; women who put on make-up and parents
who abandon their child; the man who falls
down his own well at night, slaves who groom
horses and clean the drains; people who teach
their parrots to make jokes and barbers who
work with hair piling up around their feet. You
can experience Augustine's world by reading the
sermons which he preached in such abundance
and which drew crowds to the cathedral in

Hippo. You can enter his mental world by realising that he contributed to civic life there as devotedly as he engaged in theological debate with the Church's foes.

The Donatists – a controversy about church order
So who were these foes and why was it important to get to grips with them? In Hippo Augustine did his most substantial theological work, thinking and writing the Church to a new place. His own journey to truth with its routes through heresy and other by-ways, gives his writings real authority. But equally his experience marked him; he did not write out of an emotionally neutral set of circumstances or ideas, but as a poacher turned gamekeeper.

He found himself in mid life dealing with the interpretation of scripture, the meaning of the sacraments, the exposition of doctrine as well as the mass of administrative tasks expected of a bishop. He spent a huge amount of time writing letters on behalf of individuals, on the advocacy which prominent people took on in that structured society. He began a major work on the

Trinity which would take him years to finish. But the major crisis that faced him was the Donatist schism.

Now Augustine had grown up knowing all about the Donatists as they were a group which existed only in North Africa. They took their name from a man called Donatus of Cava Nigra. Under the persecution of Diocletian in 303 Christians were made to give up their religious books. Some would and some refused. People took sides on this issue and soon the Christian Church was divided. Augustine was aware that a former bishop of Carthage, Caecilian, had tried to suppress the over-enthusiasm for martyrdom that had gripped the Donatists there, and to break the power of confessors. These were people who had been arrested rather than give up their sacred texts. Once in prison they acquired a following. They were believed by many to have unique divine authority given by their suffering and example. It was even thought that they could forgive sins.

Caecilian took action; he advised moderation. So the Donatists spread a rumour about him. He was suspected of collusion or collaboration with the state. Had he too handed over the Bible and other sacred books of the church to the authorities, when required to do so by edicts issued under the Emperor Diocletian? Whose side was he on? His election as bishop was opposed by the appointment of a rival bishop and the worst happened. Feelings ran so high that the church split into two factions: the non-rigorists, called Catholics, who supported Caecilian, and their opponents, the Donatists, as the rigorists came to be known. This was a perceived heresy with a modern ring, for Donatist traditionalists could always claim right on their side by making a bid to the authority of history, while the Catholics struggled to work out something new.

What was the attitude of the State? The imperial government did not respond well to the hysteria of the Donatists and their sectarian suspicion of civic authority. Frankly they were annoyed. The Donatists appealed to the emperor against the Catholics in 313 – ironically, given their views on church and state relations. Constantine granted them two hearings, then he got fed up with their rantings and sent them all home. Subsequently he investigated again and came to the conclusion that the Donatists were in the wrong. It is not difficult to see why. The Donatists were hugely intolerant and intemperate in their language. They were not interested in unity, which was Constantine's greatest need.

The issue was about betrayals and counter-betrayals. Trying to rebuild the church, appoint bishops and carry on as normal was difficult while accusations were flying around. Had sacred books been surrendered, or held on to by dubious means? The status of Bishop Caecilian, a hero to the Catholics and a demon to the Donatists, was a growing cause of disturbance. The Donatists thought Catholic baptism was tainted: 'He who receives faith from the faithless, receives not faith but guilt.' They also had a terrorist wing – the horrible Circumcellions who lived round the tomb of the Donatist martyrs and were outlaws, bandits and trouble makers.

At first Augustine took a liberal view on the Donatists, believing that they should not be compelled to submit, trying to win them over by persuasion, and encouraging the civic magistrates to be therapeutic rather than vindictive in their treatment of them. But the authorities' view was that tough measures were necessary, as the religious conflict spilled over into civilian life. Over time Augustine's view hardened. He came to agree with the state. He saw that schism is a basic failure of charity, and moreover that the Donatist church, because it was confined to North Africa, was a church cut off from the rest of the world. His own experience of a universal church was based on his travels in Carthage, Rome and Milan. As a son of Empire, he liked unity and the order it represented. That is the basis upon which he took issue with this group, despite their protests of purity.

In support of his attack, he quoted St Cyprian writing on schism. Now this was a confusing tactic as Cyprian was the theological hero of the Donatists. But Augustine had come to believe that the visible church would always be a mixed body, 'wheat and tares together sown unto joy or sorrow grown' – the moment of judgment was not in this world, not at the moment when the

PART TWO

lapsed or apostate were interrogated and found
guilty, but at the throne of God. The Donatists
had to be integrated; they could not separate
themselves from the body of believers. This is an
insight with a contemporary ring. Fragmentation
– even in the name of purity of doctrine –
ultimately harms the church. Charity makes
greater claims on our loyalty than any other
virtue.

So Augustine took action. He invoked the
civil authorities against the Donatists, finding a
theological justification for what he was doing in
the gospel story of the great banquet, where the
host sends his messengers into the highways and
byways to 'compel them to come in'. All is grace,
all that we do that is good comes from the grace
of God and not from ourselves. He convinced
himself that to compel the Donatists was in their
best interests. And in some ways he was right.
The rigidity and intemperance of their language
were not really in the spirit of Catholic
Christianity. But then perhaps neither was the
persecution of the Donatists by the Catholics,
leading as it inexorably did to a perception that

37

'error has no (human) rights', an understanding which would introduce to the church both the Inquisition and the stake. Augustine is judged by this controversy. In his anxiety to serve the church well, he showed little of the Catholic spirit of openness with which God had led his own restless heart to a place of rest. We are left wondering if Augustine the sinner was not a more interesting character than Augustine the saint. For the saint, the teacher, the guardian of orthodoxy plays from the back foot. His is a defensive position and it easily makes absolutist claims.

Augustine did not succeed in crushing Donatism, though it was virtually banned by law in 412. In the event the state could achieve what the church had failed to do.

Pelagians – a controversy about dogma
As a young man Augustine had wrestled with philosophical questions. The struggle with the Donatists was about church order. Now he was to think about dogma. The issue in question was one dear to his heart: in his disputes with

Pelagius he was thinking about the nature of evil in the human heart. For his sense that there was something radically adrift with the human will was developed through his involvement in what came to be called the Pelagian controversy. Once again Augustine's thinking was to be refined through engagement with people and ideas which he would never have chosen, but which drew his attention and then engaged the ferocious power of his mind.

Pelagius was a British-born monk, the son of a Roman civil servant, who had settled in Rome. When Rome fell to the Goths in 410, he travelled to Africa and then on to Jerusalem. He was a teacher and missionary among the aristocratic classes, urging active resistance to excessive wealth and injustice. He was a passionate and a generous man. It was inevitable that his path should cross with that of Augustine because both men were concerned to work out why people do wrong. How could Rome fall? How could things turn out so badly? Is it because we are born with a tendency to evil or because we do not live up to our own highest ideals and those God has for us? While studying in Rome, he was influenced by the Eastern tradition of optimism about humanity, from Origen and others who emphasised the freedom of the will. People could choose good; they were not programmed by original sin to live a fallen life of sin and shame. He was convinced that human beings are capable of fulfilling the commandments of Christ, of making a response of the will to God's goodness.

The image which comes to mind is of a chariot racing towards God, its driver eager and anxious to pursue the will of God, but driven essentially by the power of the horses' hooves and the skill of the charioteer. Pelagius had a reformer's instincts. He was irritated by Augustine's prayer in the *Confessions*: 'Give what you command and command what you will.' It sounded to him as though Augustine was passive and inactive in God's hands. To say 'all is grace' seemed to him to deny our own active collaboration in the life of faith. It sounded too easy and seemed to suggest that grace is uncomfortably like a kind of divine bribery, and not worthy of God. Pelagius did not go so far as to claim that we make our own salvation, rather he insisted that God helps us help ourselves.

So where does evil come from? Why is it that we do wrong? What about Adam and the possibility that we bear a faulty spiritual gene, as Augustine seemed to suggest? Pelagius believed that we tend to follow Adam's example, not that we are somehow born defective. He taught that we can fulfil God's destiny for us by responding to God's commandments, collaborating with him in our re-creation. He saw death as a biological necessity, not a punishment. Underneath the difference is a different estimate of human status before God. Augustine believed in original sin. He thought that we were marked with the tendency to do wrong because we are part of a fallen human race. He taught that the fall of Adam was not a mistake that could be put right, but a cosmic catastrophe. The evidence of the tragic nature of the fall was all over our moral behaviour. Left to ourselves we will always choose perversely. Is this unbearably gloomy, or, from the vantage point of a further fifteen hundred years of human history, is it all too

recognisable and an explanation of so much that
has gone wrong?

Augustine's argument with Pelagianism rum-
bled on for years. The Pelagians baited him and
in response he gradually worked out the doctrine
of human depravity which is forever associated
with him. There are those who argue that it was
Augustine's sense of guilt which now became
spelled out in a theology. For he wrote com-
pellingly about evil, about sin, and elaborated a
doctrine of original sin which has stamped the
Church's consciousness ever since. But equally
there are those who would say that the doctrine
of grace which he developed offers far more
hope for the human heart than the bland
promises of Pelagius. For the undertow of evil is
so considerable that the charioteer image does
not really work. If anything, a different image
altogether is offered by a more modern sport
than charioteering. The water-skier, poised on
blades that skim across the water, is drawn along
by the power of the boat which goes on ahead.
God, like that boat, is the source of power which
draws one on. The skier co-operates with grace

by hanging on for dear life and using skill and daring in the pursuit of the boat. That is how we are to be with God: energised by grace, skillful and daring in all we do in faith and hope and love.

Augustine already believed, and had written in the *Confessions*, that humankind stands under the righteous judgment of God and can only be saved by the mercy of God's grace. This was his own experience and he believed in it from the bottom of his heart. Monica's prayers had thrown him on the immensity of God's mercy. So, as he saw it, baptism is not just the assurance of God's love and forgiveness; it actively destroys the corruption of the soul, and shows that God's grace is sovereign and prior to human will. This was the significance of infant baptism, because God elects the saved before they are conscious enough to choose. He believed that Pelagianism was a kind of horribly misguided Stoic human-ism, whereby people would do good just by trying hard. In response Augustine was accused by his enemies of being the Manichee who does not change his spots but who was locked into a pessimism about humanity which was profoundly anti-Christian.

Nowadays there are scholars who think that Augustine was wrong for the right reasons and that Pelagius was right for the wrong reasons. For once again this debate is a contemporary one, with those who favour a doctrine of original blessing pitted against those who continue to experience the need for a doctrine of original sin. Much of modern spirituality tries to bolster up a sense of the individual's specialness and blessedness before God. It preaches a benign message about forgiveness and – inevitably perhaps, in a world as fragmented and vulnerable as our own – tries to tell people that they are all right. Meanwhile many people experience the churches' teaching and sacramental practice as trying to sound benign but actually proclaiming just the kind of bleak message which we rightly identify with Augustine's teaching on sin and evil. How can orthodoxy triumph? There are those who would argue that we need to rediscover Augustine's doctrine of grace, for it alone can make us acknowledge our sinfulness

and need for God by singing from our hearts, as
he did:

> Great are you, O Lord, and exceedingly worthy
> of praise; your power is immense, and your wis-
> dom beyond reckoning. And so we humans,
> who are a due part of your creation, long to
> praise you – we who carry our mortality about
> with us, carry the evidence of our sin and with
> it the proof that you thwart the proud. Yet these
> humans, due part your creation as they are, still
> do long to praise you. You arouse us so that
> praising you may bring us joy, because you have
> made us and drawn us to yourself, and our heart
> is unquiet until it rests in you. (*Confessions* I,1.)

Church and state

Augustine's final contribution to western thought
was the political theory he developed about the
relationship of church and state. The sack of
Rome in 410 by Alaric the Visigoth was a water-
shed, a shameful assault on the comforting idea
that God was bringing the empire to fulfilment
through the union of emperor and church. These

were troubled times. Augustine's view is completely the opposite to the optimism of Eusebius of Caesarea, the court historian who had written up the age of Constantine in such glowing terms, presenting it as a manifestation of divine grace, with the emperor starring in the lead role. For Augustine there were two realities, the City of this World and the City of God. Both are here together interwoven and the true citizenship is not revealed until the last judgment. The apocalyptic strain which belongs to North African theology comes to life, and Augustine develops a theology of suspended judgment. Political life is possible, and necessary, but one cannot prejudge or make assumptions about which form of government is God's will. The two cities grow secretly through time.

In nature, too, there is a yearning for God, that all things come from God and revolve around him, that the unfolding of creation craves for its return and rest. This rest is particularly important in his thinking about the Trinity. Augustine saw footprints of the Trinity all over creation but especially in humanity, made in

God's image. Even in his *Confessions*, he had written: 'I could wish that people would but consider these three things that are in themselves … namely to Be, to Know, and to Will. For indeed I am, and I know, and I will. I am, both knowing and willing. I know myself both to be and to will. And I am willing both to be and to know.'

Augustine grappled with the idea that there are three Persons in the one God of the Christian tradition. To help him think this through, he reflected on the relationship of our own memory, understanding and will, attributes of the Godhead which, as he saw it, mark us with the identity of the Blessed Trinity. He wrote:

> I do not say that the Father is memory, the Son understanding, and the Holy Ghost will … I do not say that these things are to be equated by analogy as it were to the Holy Trinity, that is to say are to be arranged according to some exact rule of comparison. This I do not say. But what do I say? See, I have discovered in you three things which are exhibited separately, whose operation is inseparable; and of these three

every single name is produced by the three together; yet does this name belongs not to the three but to some one of those three. In the Trinity then, believe what you cannot not see, if in yourself you have heard, and seen, and retained it.

The authority of human experience and self-understanding become an absolute for Augustine. As he wrote, 'The whole Trinity is revealed to us in its works.'

Now there are gains and there are losses when a person's theology is drawn from experience as troubled as Augustine's. The church has gained hugely from his desire and willingness to grapple with big ideas, to risk exploring human evil by examining his own restless heart. He left theological reflection at a different place from where he found it. He told us more about ourselves, more about God and more about the image of God we bear within the human psyche. Had his not been a journey of personal discovery, had he not learnt from his errors and his own sins, the canvas of his thinking might not have stretched so far. His legacy might not have been so considerable, but equally his influence would have been less divisive to future generations. For terrible things have been done in Augustine's name, just as they have been in the name of the Lord who battered on his restless heart, and to whom he submitted in love. It was the man who heard the child's voice calling out, 'Take and read; take and read', who later wrote, 'Nothing conquers except truth: the victory of truth is charity.'

As Augustine grew older his vision simplified. He wrote, 'Let your old age be childlike, and your childhood like old age; that is, so that neither may your wisdom be with pride, nor your humility without wisdom'. The enemies who had so bothered him because they attacked his deepest beliefs, came and went. He continued to do battle on behalf of the church and, when he died, he did so in harness, with words of repentance on his lips:

This is what he did in his last illness: for he had ordered the four psalms of David that deal with penance to be copied out. From his sick-bed he could see these sheets of paper every day, hanging on his walls, and would read them, crying constantly and deeply. And, lest his attention be distracted from this in any way, almost ten days before his death, he asked that none should come in to see him, except in those hours when the doctors would come to examine him or his meals were brought. This was duly observed: and so he had all that stretch of time to pray.

— *Possidins,* Life of Augustine

Augustine died on 28 August 430, the day on which the church now celebrates his feast. The orderly world of Empire which had nurtured him was in tatters. The Vandals had got as far as North Africa. Augustine's legacy to the church would now be tested and proved to be correct, for the city of God would still unfold itself amid the confusion of a hostile world and, to this day, we do not know its boundaries. God's work is never done.

PART TWO

Lord, renew in your church the spirit you gave St Augustine. Filled with this spirit, may we thirst for you alone as the fountain of wisdom and seek you as the source of eternal love.

We ask this through our Lord Jesus Christ, your Son, who lives and reigns with you and the Holy Spirit, one God, for ever and ever.

— Collect for the feast of St Augustine,
Roman Missal

PART THREE

Prayers and Writings

PART THREE

Prayers and Writings

These quotations are from Augustine's Confessions, *commentaries on the scriptures, theological writings and sermons. They give a rich portrait of the workings of his mind and the depth of his faith. They identify his as a restless and a confessing heart.*

Too late have I come to love you, O beauty, so ancient and yet so new; too late have I come to love you. For behold, you were within me, and I without; and I searched for you there, and in a desperate way I threw myself on the things of your creation, which you made so beautiful. You were indeed with me, but I was not with you. Things withheld me from you, yet had you not made them, they would not have existed. You called and cried out, and so you broke through my deafness. You shone out and glowed, and so you drove away my blindness. You breathed fragrance on me, and I drew in my breath, yet still I pant after you. I tasted you, and still I hunger and thirst for more. You touched me, and I burn with the desire to enjoy you.

– *Confessions X, 27*

I beg you to consider that there is nothing in this life, and especially in our own day, more easy and pleasant and acceptable to others than the office of a bishop or priest or deacon, if its duties be discharged in a mechanical way, but nothing more worthless and deplorable and meet for chastisement in the sight of God; and, on the other hand, that there is nothing in this life, and especially in our own day, more difficult, toilsome and hazardous than the office of a bishop or priest or deacon, but nothing more blessed in the sight of God, if our service be in accordance with our Captain's orders. But how that is to be done I learned neither in my boyhood nor in my youth, and just as I had begun to learn, I was compelled by reason of my sins to assume the second place at the helm, although I did not know how to hold an oar.

But I imagine that it was my Lord's intention to chastise me because I was bold enough to rebuke many sailors for their faults, as though I were a wiser and a better man, before experience had taught me the nature of their work. So, on being sent into their midst, I then began to realise how presumptuous were my rebukes, although even before that time I had concluded that this occupation was fraught with great hazards. This was the cause of the tears which some of the brethren noticed me shedding when I was newly ordained; they said all they could to console me, but, though their intentions were good, their words had no bearing whatever on my trouble, as they did not know the reasons for my grief.

– Letter no. 21: to Bishop Valerius

I call upon you, O God, the Truth, in whom, by whom, and through whom those things are true which are true in every respect.

God, the Wisdom, in whom and by whom and through whom those things are wise which anywhere are wise.

God, the true and highest life, in whom and by whom and through whom those things live which anywhere live truly and supremely.

God, the Beatitude, in whom and by whom and through whom all things are happy which anywhere are happy.

God, the Good and the beautiful, in whom and by whom and through whom those things are good and beautiful which anywhere are good and beautiful.

God, the intelligible Light, in whom, and by whom, and through whom those things intelligibly shine which anywhere intelligibly shine.

God, whose knowledge is a whole universe of which the senses have no knowledge.

God, for whose kingdom law is assigned even to those realms.

God, from whom to be turned away is to fall,

to whom to be turned again is to rise again, in whom to abide is to stand secure.

God, from whom to depart is to die, to whom to return is to be restored to life, in whom to dwell is to live.

God, whom no one loses unless deceived, whom no one seeks unless stirred to do so, whom no one finds unless made pure.

God, whom to forsake is the same as to perish; whom to strive for is the same as to live; whom to see is the same as to possess.

God to whom faith urges us, hope raises us, charity joins us.

— *Soliloquy, I, 1, 3*

God, whom all things serve, that serve; to whom every virtuous soul submits; by whose laws the poles rotate, the stars complete their courses, the sun oversees the day, the moon rules the night: the whole universe, day by day by the alternation of light and darkness; month by month by the waxings and wanings of the moon; year by year by due succession of spring, summer, autumn and winter; cycle by cycle as the sun completes its appointed path; orbit by orbit as the stars return to their place of rising, maintains, as far as sensible matter permits, an enduring harmony.

God, by whose eternal laws the unstable motion of mutable things is not allowed to be disturbed, but by the restraining force of recurring cycles is ever called back to a similitude of stability: by whose laws the will of the soul is free, and to the good rewards are given, to the evil punishments by wholly necessary connection.

God, from whom flow to us all good things, by whom all evil things are kept from us.

God, above whom is nothing, beyond whom is nothing, without whom is nothing.

God, under whom all is, in whom all is, with whom all is.

– Soliloquy, I, 1, 4

The Lord is good and everywhere his mercy is shed abroad, which comforts us with your love in him. How greatly he loves those who believe and hope in him and who love both him and one another, and what blessings he stores up for them to enjoy hereafter. Strive more earnestly to disseminate harmony among yourselves than to encourage fault-finding, for just as vinegar corrodes a vessel if it remain too long in it, so anger corrodes the heart if it linger on to another day.

– Letter no. 220: to Felicitas and Rusticus

To our hearts God is light, and sound, and odour, and food; and he is all of these things for the reason that he is none of these things, and he is none of these things for the reason that he is the Creator of all these things. He is light to our hearts, to whom we say, 'In thy light we shall see light' (Psalm 35.10). To our hearts he is sound, to whom we say, 'To my hearing thou shalt give joy and gladness' (Psalm 1.10). Odour to our hearts is he of whom it is said, 'We are the good odour of Christ' (2 Corinthians 2.15). But if you seek food, because you are fasting, 'Blessed are they that hunger and thirst after justice (Matthew 5.6). But of the Lord Jesus himself it is said that he 'is made unto us wisdom and justice' (1 Corinthians 1.30). Behold the feast is prepared. Justice is Christ and it nowhere is wanting; it is not prepared by cooks. It is not like foreign fruits brought to us by merchants from lands beyond the sea; he is food which everyone can savour who has a healthy palate; he is food which restores and does not fail; he is food which fills the hungry, yet remains undiminished.

— Sermon 28, 2–5

In the land of the living we ought to have a root. Let our root be there. That root is out of sight; its fruits may be seen, the root cannot be seen. Our root is our charity; our fruits are our works. It is needful that your works proceed from charity; then is your root in the land of the living.

– On the Psalms 51, 12

Thus the love which is of God and is God is specially the Holy Spirit, through whom is spread abroad in our hearts the charity of God by which the whole Trinity will make its habitation within us. And therefore the Holy Spirit, God though he is, is most rightly called also the gift of God; and the special sense of that gift must be charity, which brings us to God, and without which no other gift of God, whatever it may be, can bring us to God.

– On the Trinity 18, 32

Let the Lord your God be your hope. Hope for nothing else from the Lord your God, but let the Lord your God himself be your hope. For many people hope to obtain riches from God, and many people hope for perishable and transitory honours; in short, they hope to get from God's hands almost anything else, except God himself. But seek after God, despising all other things, make your way to him. Forget things, remember him. Leave other things behind and stretch forth to him. It is he who is leading you to your goal. Therefore, let him be your hope as he is leading you and guiding you to your destination. He who made heaven and earth is more beautiful than all. He who made all things is better than all. He who made the beautiful things is more beautiful than all. He who made the mighty things is himself mightier. He who made the great things is himself greater. He will be to you everything which you love. Learn to love the Creator in the creature, and in the work the one who made it.

– On the Psalms 39, 7, 8

Eternal life is the actual knowledge of the truth. See then how perverse and preposterous are those who imagine that their teachings of the knowledge of God will make us perfect, when this is the reward of those already perfect. What else, then, I ask, have we to do but first to love with complete charity, him whom we desire to know?

— *On Death Eccl. I, 25, 47*

The striving after God is therefore the desire of beatitude, the attainment of God is beatitude itself. We seek to attain God by loving him; we attain to him, not by becoming entirely what he is, but in nearness to him, and in wonderful and sensible contact with him, and in being inwardly illuminated and occupied by his truth and holiness. He is light itself; it is given to us to be illuminated by that light.

– On Death Eccl. I, 11, 18

The whole nature of the universe about us, to which we also belong, proclaims that it has a most excellent Creator, who has given to us a mind and natural reason, whereby to see that things living are to be preferred to things not living, things that have sense to things that are insensible, things that have understanding to things that have not, things immortal to things mortal, things powerful to things impotent, things just to things unjust, things beautiful to things unsightly, things good to things evil, the incorruptible to the corruptible, the immutable to the mutable, the invisible to the visible, the incorporeal to the corporeal, things happy to things miserable. And hence, since without doubt we place the Creator above created things, we must needs confess that he both lives in the highest sense, and perceives and understands all things, and that he cannot die, or suffer corruption, or be changed; and that he is not a body but a spirit; of all the most powerful, the most just, the most beautiful, most good, most blessed.

– On the Trinity 15, 4, 6

For we cultivate God, and God cultivates us. But we do not so cultivate God as to make him any better thereby. For our cultivation is the labour of an adoring heart, not of the hands. He cultivates us as the husbandman tills his field. As he cultivates us, so he makes us better, just as the husbandman by tilling his field makes it better. And the fruit that he seeks in us is that we may cultivate him. The tillage he practises on us is that he does not cease to root out by his word the evil seeds from our heats, to open, as it were, our heart by the plough of his word, to plant the seed of his precepts, to wait for the fruit of piety. For when we have so received that tillage in our heart as to cultivate him well, we are not ungrateful to our Husbandman, but yield the fruit in which he rejoices. And our fruit does not make him the richer, but us the happier.

— *Sermon 87, 1, 1*

For the very fact that we are not yet with God, the very fact that we are living amid trials and difficulties, that we cannot be without fear, is tribulation, since there is not that peace which is promised us. Anyone who has not found this tribulation in this pilgrimage, does not think of going home to heaven. This is tribulation. Surely now we do good works when we give bread to the hungry, a home to the stranger, and so on. This too is tribulation. For we find pitiful objects upon whom we show pity; and the misery of these pitiful objects makes us compassionate. How much better it would be for you to be where you find no hungry people to feed, no strangers to take in, no one naked to clothe, no sick people to visit, no litigant to reconcile. For in that place all things are of the highest degree, are true, are holy, are eternal. Our bread there is justice, our drink wisdom, our garment immortality, our house everlasting in the heavens, our strength immortality. There is no death there, no strife, but in their place, peace, repose, justice.

– *On the Psalms 44, 22*

Understanding is the reward of faith. Therefore do not seek to understand that you may believe, but believe so that you may understand.

– On the Gospel of St John 29, 6

For in the City we shall be where God is our good, God is our light, God is our bread, God is our life. In him we shall find every good – whatever good thing of ours there is, absence from which now troubles us.

– On the Psalms 37, 28

To go through life planning journeys that cannot
be undertaken without disturbance and trouble
does not become one who is planning for that
last journey we call death; with it alone, as you
are aware, should our real plans be concerned. It
is God's gift to some few men, whom he has
appointed to rule over churches, not only to
await death manfully but even to desire it
eagerly, and to undertake the toil of those other
journeys without vexation. But in my opinion
neither those who are impelled to such administrative tasks by love of worldly position, nor
those who, though occupying no public post,
hunger for a life of affairs, have been granted the
great boon of acquiring amid their clamour and
their restless running hither and thither that
familiarity with death that we are seeking; both
classes might have become godly in retirement.
If this be untrue, then I am of all men, I won't
say the most foolish, but certainly the most
slothful, for I cannot relish and enjoy that real
boon, unless I obtain release from work and
worry. Complete withdrawal from the turmoil of
transitory things is, believe me, essential before a

man can develop that fearlessness in the face of death which is based neither on insensibility nor on foolhardy presumption, neither on the desire for empty glory nor on superstitious credulity. It is that which is the origin of that solid joy with which no pleasure from any transitory source is in any way to be compared.

– Letter no. 10: to Nebridius

Peace will be there, perfect peace will be there. You will be where you wish to be, but you will not depart from God. You will be where you wish to be, but where you go you will have God. You will be with him, from whom you are blessed, for ever.

— *Sermon 242, 8, 11*

But yet, when I love you, what is it I love? Not the beauty of anybody, not the order of time, not the clearness of this light that so gladdens our eyes, nor the harmony of sweet songs of every kind, not the scent of flowers, or spices of aromatic odours, not manna, nor honey, nor limbs delightful in the embrace of flesh and blood. Not these things do I love, in loving my God. Yet I do love a kind of light, a kind of voice, a kind of odour, a kind of food, a kind of embracing, when I love my God, who is the light, the voice, the odour, the food, the embracing of my inward self; when that light shines into my soul which is not circumscribed by any place, when that voice sounds which is not snatched away by time, when that odour pours forth which is not scattered by the air, when that food has the taste which is unconsumed by eating, when that embrace is enjoyed which is not divorced by satiety. This is what I love, when I love my God.

– Confessions X, 7, 8

For this seventh day will be our sabbath, whose end will not be any evening, but the Lord's day, an eternal eighth day. For that day has been sanctified by the resurrection of Christ to prefigure the eternal rest not only of the spirit but also of the body.

Where we shall rest and we shall see; we shall see and we shall love; we shall love and we shall praise. That is what shall be in the end without end. For what is our end but to arrive at the kingdom which has no end?

I think that I have now, by God's help, discharged my duty in completing this great task. Those who think I have written too little or too much, must forgive me. Those who are satisfied must not thank me, but join with me in giving thanks to God. Amen. Amen.

— *The City of God 22, 30*

FURTHER READING

FURTHER READING

Augustine of Hippo, *Selected Writings*, SPCK, 1984.

Augustine of Hippo, *Confessions*, Translated by Maria Boulding OSB, Hodder & Stoughton, 1997.

David Bentley-Taylor, *Augustine: Wayward Genius*, Hodder & Stoughton, 1980.

Peter Brown, *Augustine of Hippo*, Faber & Faber, 1967.

Henry Chadwick, *Augustine*, Oxford University Press, 1986.

F. W. Farrer, *The Life of St Augustine*, Hodder & Stoughton, 1993.

Andrew Louth, *The Origins of the Christian Mystical Tradition*, Clarendon Press, 1981.